WHERE DOES MY POO GO?

JO LINDLEY

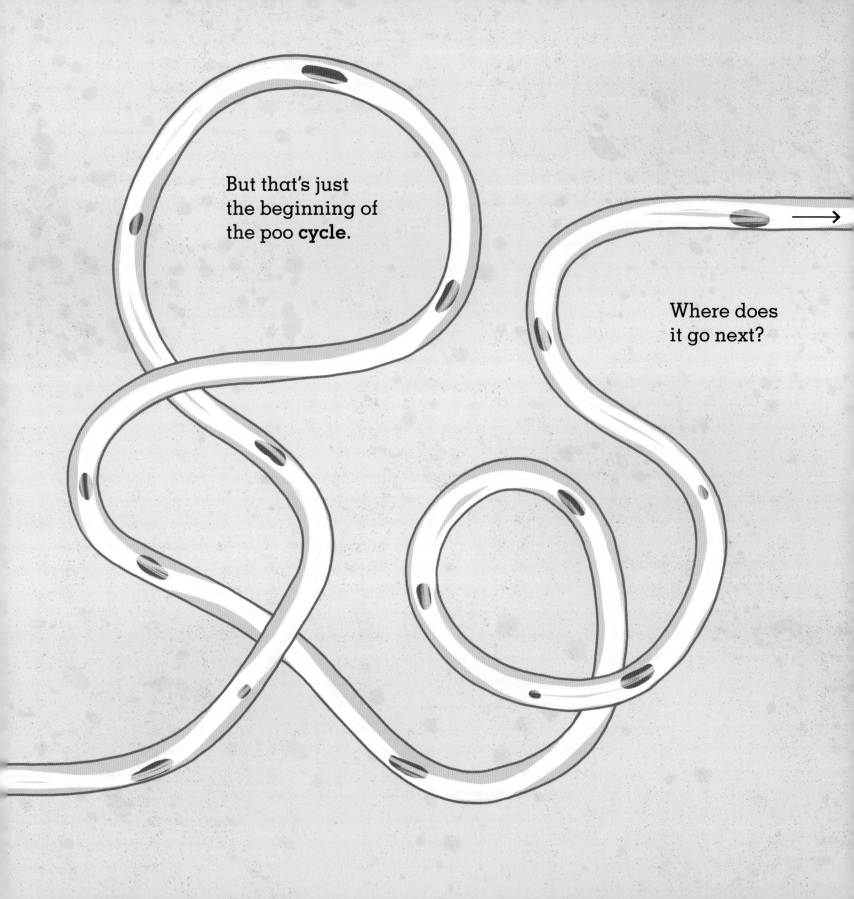

But that's just the beginning of the poo **cycle**.

Where does it go next?

It whizzes away through the pipes in your house to bigger pipes underground, known as **sewers**.

Your neighbour's poo does the same...

as does your neighbour's neighbour's poo...

SEWER

and your
neighbour's
neighbour's
neighbour's
poo!

SEWAGE

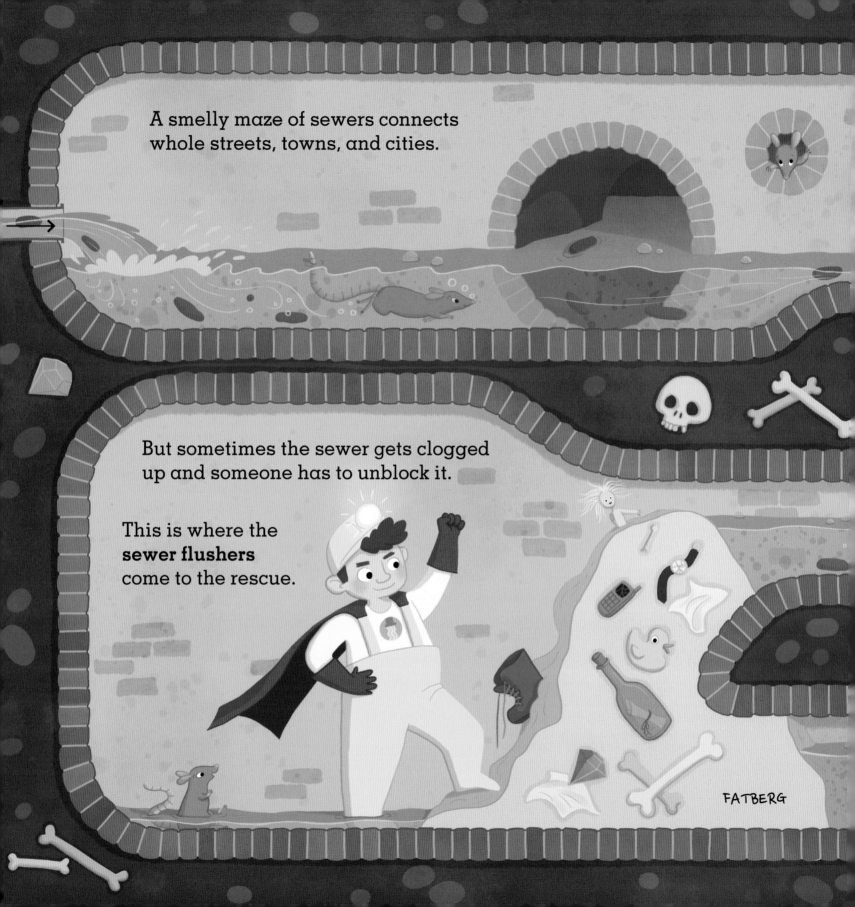

A smelly maze of sewers connects whole streets, towns, and cities.

But sometimes the sewer gets clogged up and someone has to unblock it.

This is where the **sewer flushers** come to the rescue.

FATBERG

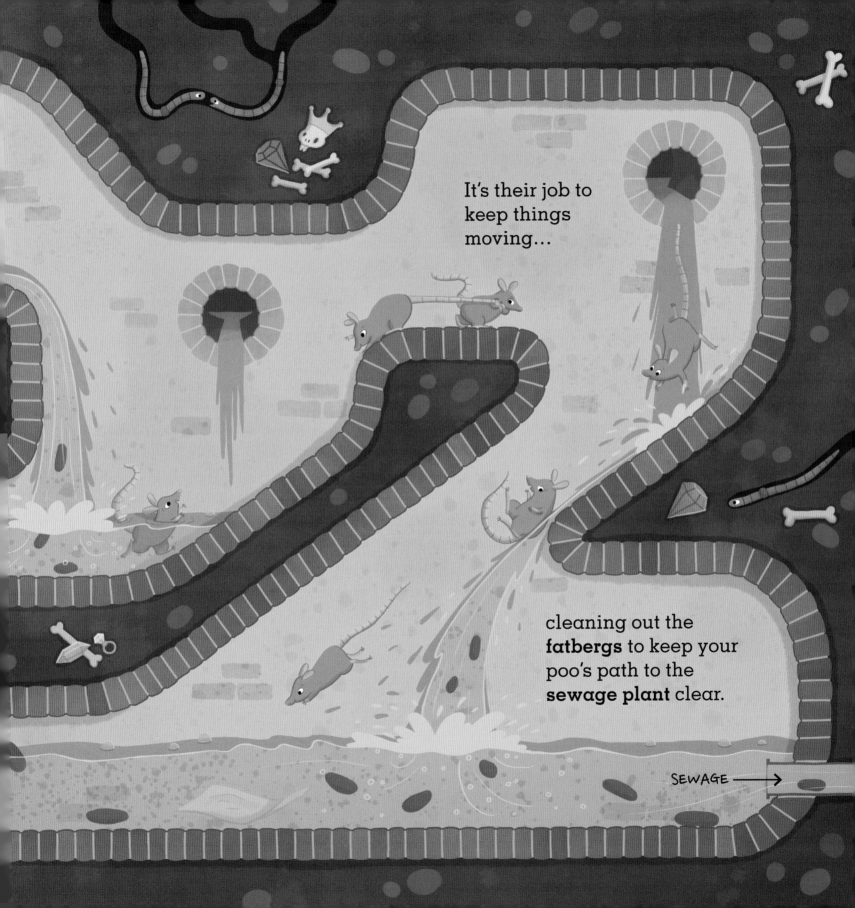

It's their job to keep things moving...

cleaning out the **fatbergs** to keep your poo's path to the **sewage plant** clear.

SEWAGE →

The dirty water arriving at the sewage plant has to be cleaned. The first step is to take out all the stuff that shouldn't have been flushed at all.

The water passes through a screen. This is a bit like a giant sieve on a moving belt, but rather than straining spaghetti, it's picking out nappies, wet wipes, and even false teeth.

SCREEN

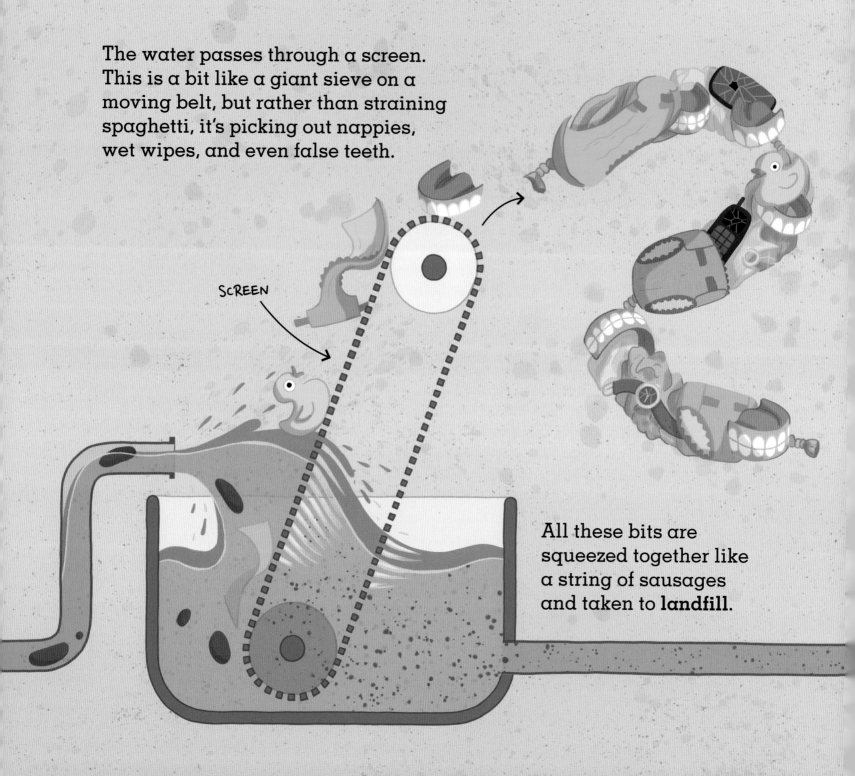

All these bits are squeezed together like a string of sausages and taken to **landfill**.

The **sewage** is pumped into a tank where the water and the poo split up.
The water rises to the top and the poo sinks to the bottom, making **sludge**.
This gloopy mess is scraped out and **recycled**.

But we'll get onto that later.
The water has a battle to
face first...

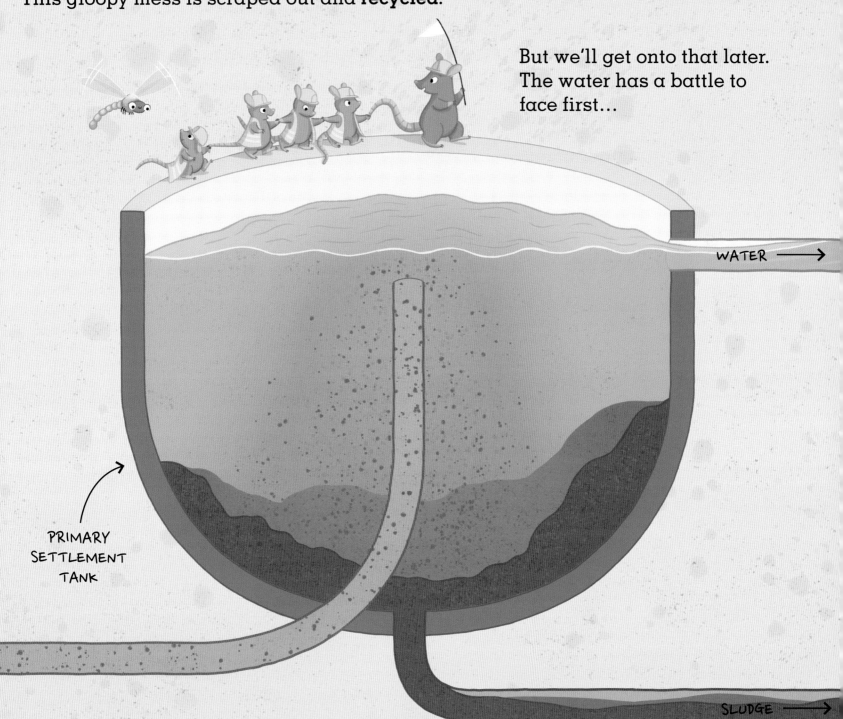

PRIMARY
SETTLEMENT
TANK

WATER ⟶

SLUDGE ⟶

the BATTLE of the BUGS!

The water may look fairly clean at this stage, but it is actually full of **bacteria**, both good and bad! Bubbles are pumped into the water, which the good bacteria ride around on. This gives them lots of energy to eat up the bad bacteria.

BIOLOGICAL
TREATMENT

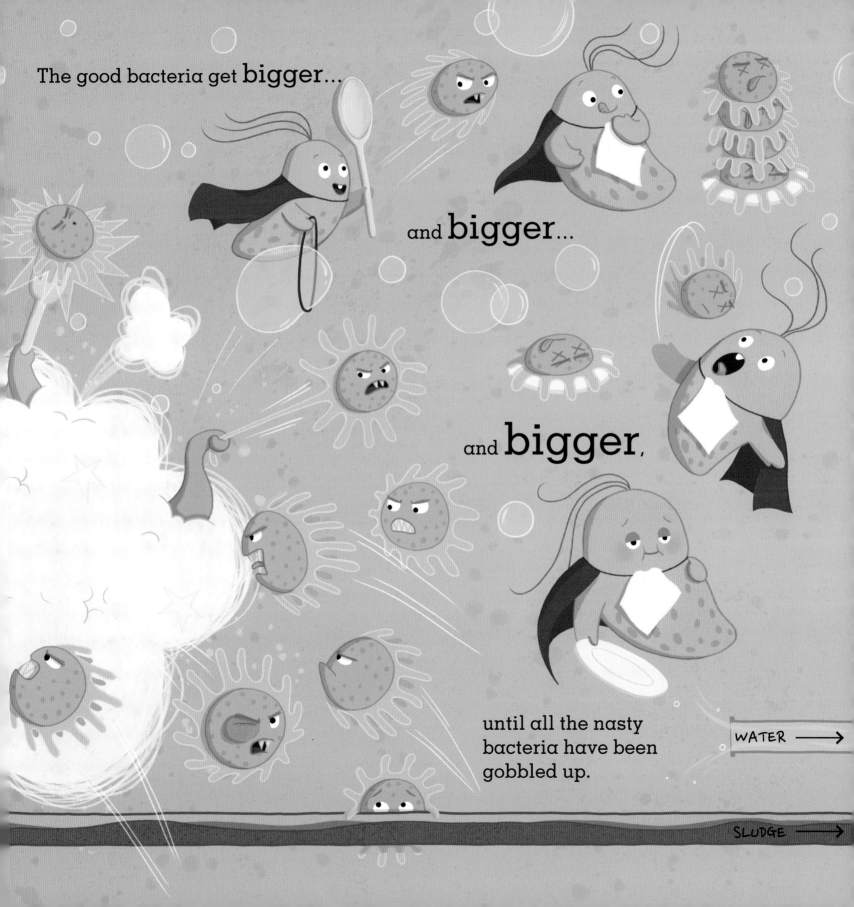

The good bacteria get **bigger**...

and **bigger**...

and **bigger**,

until all the nasty bacteria have been gobbled up.

WATER ⟶

SLUDGE ⟶

The good bacteria become so full they sink to the bottom of the next tank.

Here, they have a little rest before going back to fight another battle of the bugs. Or they join the rest of the sludge as it moves on to the next stage of the poo cycle.

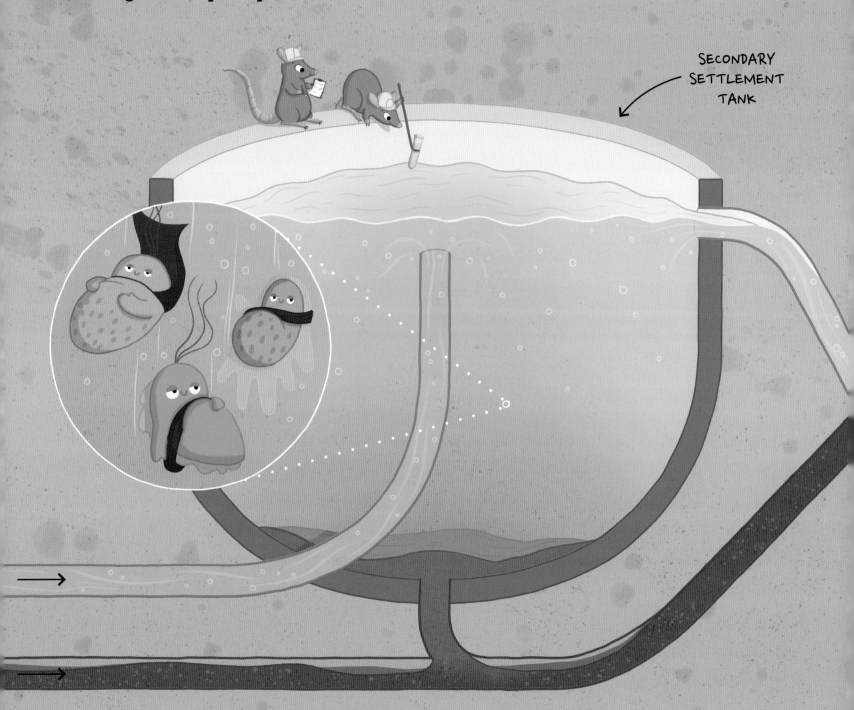

SECONDARY SETTLEMENT TANK

The sludge and the leftover bacteria are collected together in a giant pot, known as an anaerobic digester, and warmed up to almost the same temperature as your body – perfect for **digestion**.

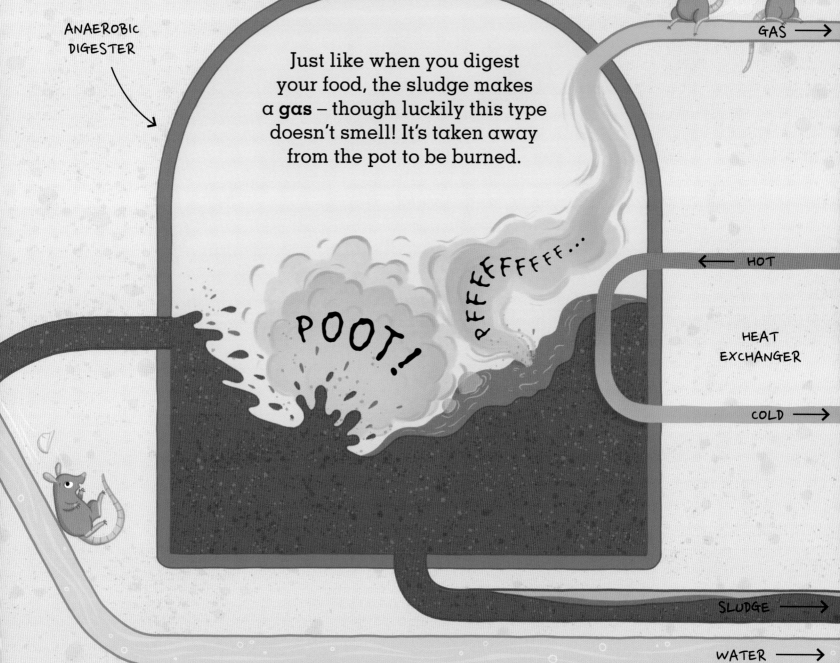

ANAEROBIC
DIGESTER

Just like when you digest your food, the sludge makes a **gas** – though luckily this type doesn't smell! It's taken away from the pot to be burned.

GAS ⟶

POOT!

PFFFFFFFF...

← HOT

HEAT
EXCHANGER

COLD ⟶

SLUDGE ⟶

WATER ⟶

When the gas is burned it makes lots and lots of heat. This can be sent back to warm up the sludge, or may even be used to make electricity at a **power plant**.

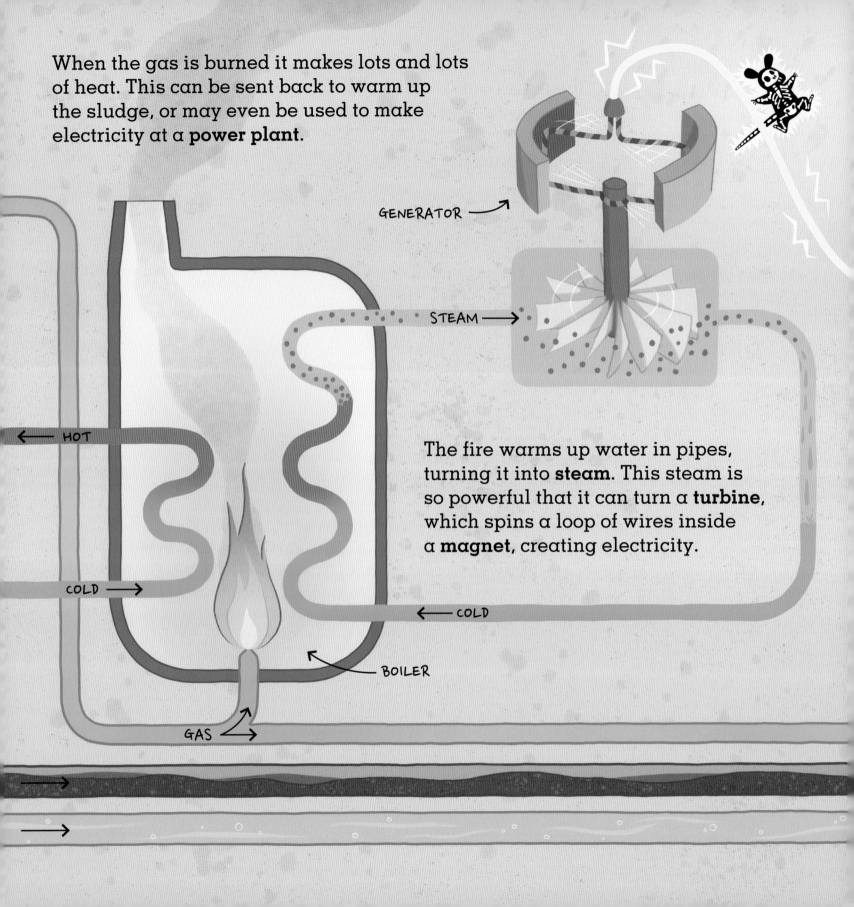

GENERATOR

STEAM →

← HOT

COLD →

The fire warms up water in pipes, turning it into **steam**. This steam is so powerful that it can turn a **turbine**, which spins a loop of wires inside a **magnet**, creating electricity.

← COLD

BOILER

GAS

The electricity can be used to power the sewage treatment plant, or wires can carry it all the way to your home to power your lights, machines, gadgets, and gizmos.

TRANSFORMER

PYLON

TRANSFORMER

METER

SMELLYVISION

That means that poo could be powering your television tonight!

GAS →

SLUDGE →

WATER →

But if the gas is cleaned so that it only contains a chemical called **methane**, it can be used for even more things.

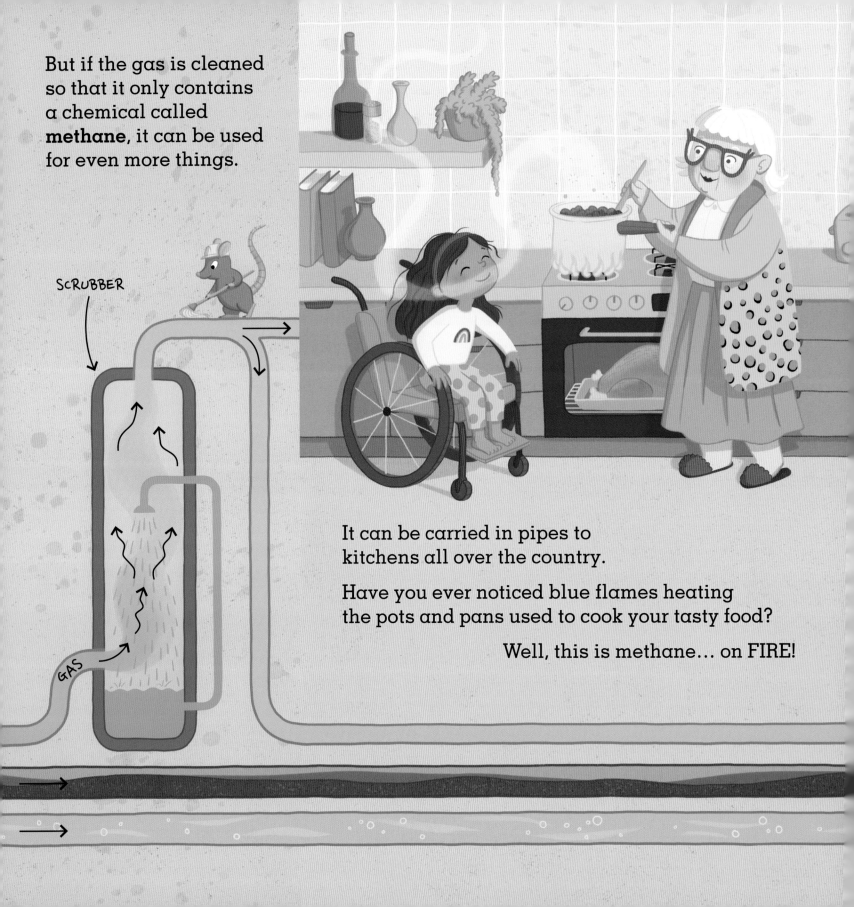

SCRUBBER

GAS

It can be carried in pipes to kitchens all over the country.

Have you ever noticed blue flames heating the pots and pans used to cook your tasty food?

Well, this is methane… on FIRE!

Or it can be used as **fuel** for vehicles and may even be powering your local bus. The best part is that methane fuel is better for the environment than normal fuel.

POO BUS

METHANE

And this is just the gas. Don't forget the...

SLUDGE ⟶

WATER ⟶

SLUDGE

FILTER
PRESS

CENTRIFUGE

This is the sludge from the digester pot. It's still full of **nutrients**, but it's too sloppy to be used just yet – the water needs to be removed. One way is to spin it really, really fast, just like a washing machine.

Any leftover water is then squeeeeeeezed out,
leaving dark and crumbly looking stuff called **cake**.

But you DON'T want to eat this cake – it would taste HORRIBLE!

This sort of cake is destined for farms.

CAKE

THE FARM

WATER ⟶

Some farmers mix cake into the soil. So before you moan about the smell of a farm, just remember – that could be the pong of your own poo!

THE FARM

Nutrients in cake feed the plants, helping them grow big and strong – just like eating healthy food does for you.

This is where we leave the poo story and return to the water.
It has an adventure to go on…

NUTRIENTS

WATER →

...because it is now clean enough to join rivers.

When the Sun warms up a river, some of
the water changes into an invisible gas.
It rises up into the sky, where it gets colder
and turns back into tiny droplets of water.

HEAT

EVAPORATION

VAPOUR

The droplets bunch up together to make clouds, which get heavier and heavier, until...

CONDENSATION

PRECIPITATION

SPLISH! SPLASH!

the droplets fall back down as rain, rejoining the river.

WATER →

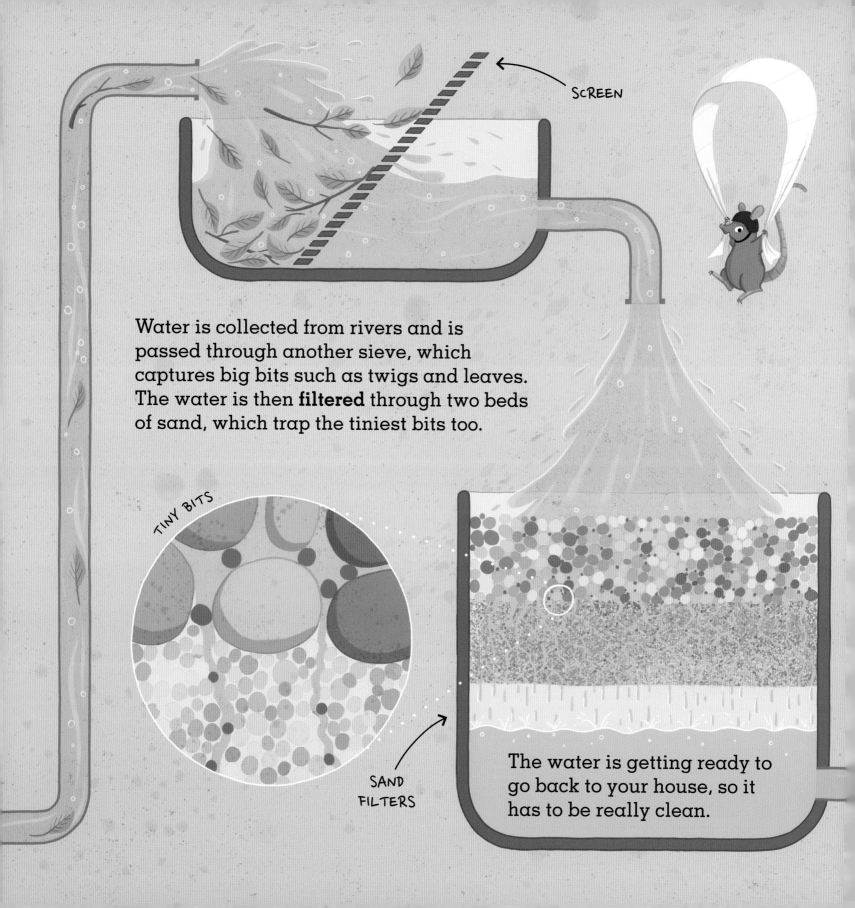

SCREEN

Water is collected from rivers and is passed through another sieve, which captures big bits such as twigs and leaves. The water is then **filtered** through two beds of sand, which trap the tiniest bits too.

TINY BITS

SAND FILTERS

The water is getting ready to go back to your house, so it has to be really clean.

One last thing is to kill any sneaky germs that might still be trying to hide in there. So the strange-smelling stuff they add to swimming pool water, called **chlorine**, is added in small amounts to the water.

SNEAKY GERMS

Now it's super-squeaky clean.

NO SWIMMING!

WATER →

FINAL TREATMENT

CHLORINE

Finally, the water is sent through a **network** of pipes all the way to your house.

So what happens to your poo is NOT MAGIC after all!

It's a very clever system that takes your poo away, uses it for energy, and brings the clean water back.

But to complete the cycle, all you have to do is press a button or a handle.

So, the next time you flush the loo,
say hello to the ghost of your old poo!

POOOOOOOOooo.....

(Now wash
your hands.)

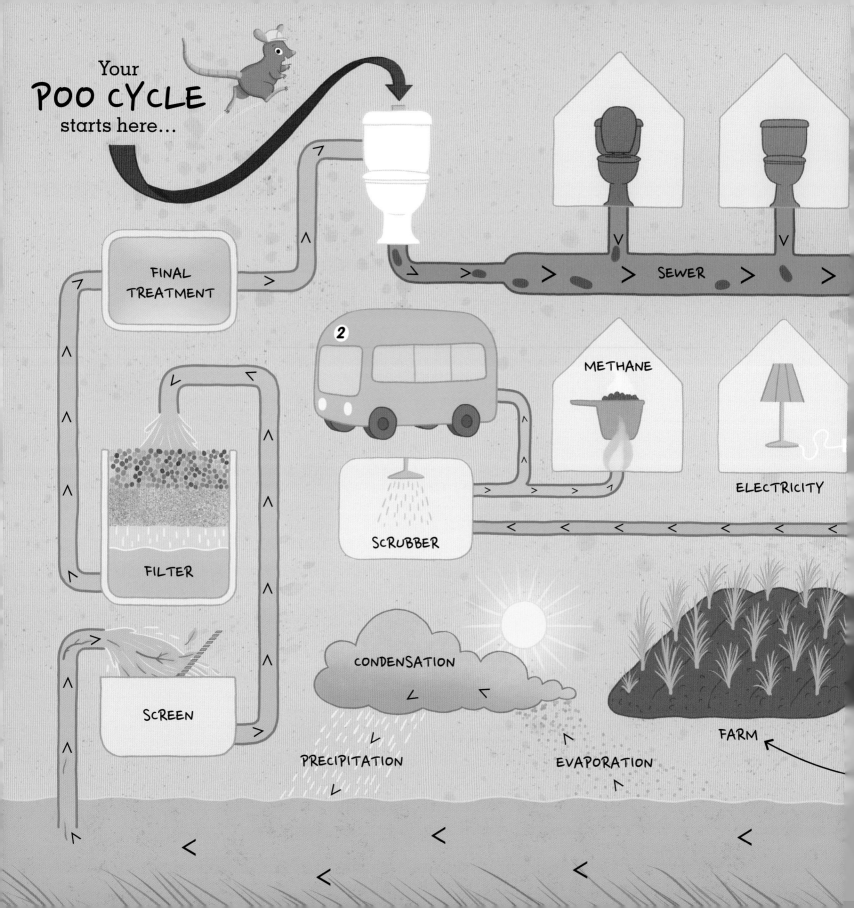

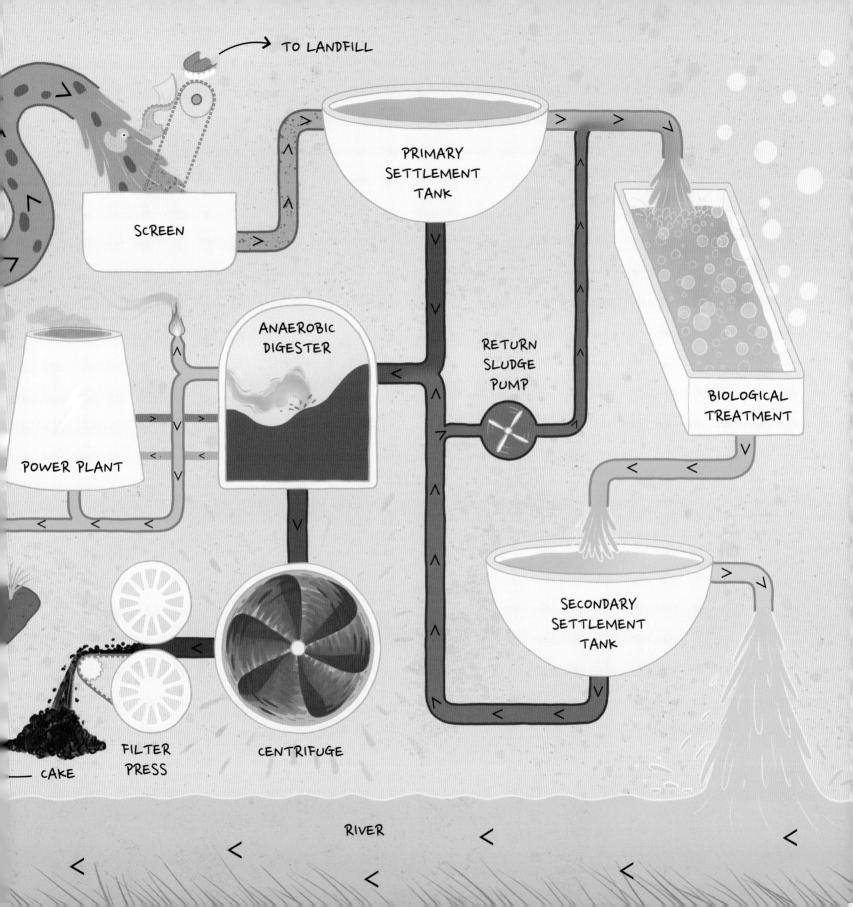

TO LANDFILL

SCREEN

PRIMARY SETTLEMENT TANK

ANAEROBIC DIGESTER

RETURN SLUDGE PUMP

BIOLOGICAL TREATMENT

POWER PLANT

SECONDARY SETTLEMENT TANK

CAKE

FILTER PRESS

CENTRIFUGE

RIVER

GLOSSARY

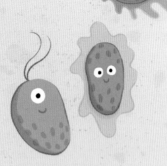

BACTERIA

A very simple form of life that's so small, it can only be seen with a microscope.

CAKE

A drier version of sludge.

CHLORINE

A chemical added to water to make it safe to drink or swim in.

17
Cl
chlorine
35.45

CYCLE

A group of actions that lead from one to the other, and circle back round to the beginning to repeat again and again.

DIGESTION

The process that breaks things down into simpler forms. For example, you eat lots of different things in one day, but once they've been digested in your tummy, they all come out as poo.

FATBERG

A huge lump of cooking fat stuck in the sewers. All sorts of strange things that should never have been flushed down the toilet get caught up in it.

FILTER

Something with lots of tiny holes in it that can be used to remove larger objects from water as it passes through.

FUEL

Something that makes energy when it is burned.

GAS

Invisible stuff floating in the air. For example, when you warm up water, it gets lots of energy, which makes it float into the air as a gas called steam.

LANDFILL

A place where rubbish is taken to be buried.

MAGNET

A metal that can pull other metals towards it.

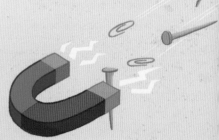

METHANE
A type of gas that is made as the sludge digests. It is similar to the smelly gas that comes out of your bottom as food is digested in your body!

NETWORK
Lots of lines or channels (such as roads or sewer pipes) connected to each other to create a huge net-like system.

NUTRIENTS
Something in cake that helps plants grow.

POWER PLANT
A factory that makes electricity.

RECYCLE
Making waste or rubbish useful again.

SEWER
Underground pipes that take used water, poo, and rainwater away from buildings and to the sewage plant.

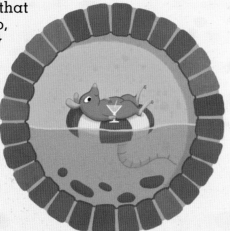

SEWER FLUSHER
A person whose job it is to clean out the fatbergs from the sewers and to keep the water and poo flowing to the sewage plant.

SEWAGE PLANT
A place that cleans the dirty water that has arrived from the sewers, and takes the poo out to be used for heat, electricity, and farms.

SLUDGE
Poo mixed with water.

STEAM
Water that has been heated up and turned into a gas.

TURBINE
A paddle that is turned by steam, water, or air.

ABOUT JO LINDLEY

Drawing was a huge part of Jo's childhood. She would burn through paper (figuratively speaking) and then wait impatiently for her parents to top up her supplies. It was tough for them to keep up with her habit! At university, art was replaced by architecture (designing buildings), and her drawings became more technical, until one happy afternoon she rediscovered the joy of doodling characters. She hasn't stopped since and now calls herself an **archistrator** (architect + illustrator).

Jo has a relatively puerile sense of humour – she wouldn't say poo jokes were her favourite, but they're a solid number two. With this in mind, along with having to spend a huge amount of time dealing with poo pipes in her architecture work, creating a book on this theme was a natural fit.

DK | Penguin Random House

Produced for DK by Plum 5

Editor Sophie Parkes
Designer Brandie Tully-Scott

Consultants William Coutts, Paul Hampton, Devendra Saroj
Publishing Manager Francesca Young
Jacket Coordinator Issy Walsh
Publishing Director Sarah Larter
Creative Director Helen Senior
Production Editor Tony Phipps
Production Controller Ena Matagic

First published in Great Britain in 2021 by
Dorling Kindersley Limited
One Embassy Gardens, 8 Viaduct Gardens,
London, SW11 7BW

The authorised representative in the EEA is
Dorling Kindersley Verlag GmbH. Arnulfstr. 124,
80636 Munich, Germany

A CIP catalogue record for this book
is available from the British Library.
ISBN: 978-0-2414-4628-7

Printed and bound in China

www.dk.com

FSC MIX
Paper | Supporting responsible forestry
FSC™ C018179

This book was made with Forest Stewardship Council™ certified paper – one small step in DK's commitment to a sustainable future.
Learn more at www.dk.com/uk/ information/sustainability